ARKANA

How to Stop Smoking Easily

Michael Blate is well known as a leading teacher and authority in the art (or science) of self-health. He has appeared on nationwide radio and television in Britain and the USA, and is the author of more than a dozen books in the field of natural health and healing without drugs or medicines, including *The Natural Healer's Acupressure Handbook: G-Jo Fingertip Technique*, *Advanced G-Jo*, *How to Heal Yourself Using Hand Acupressure*, *How to Heal Yourself Using Foot Acupressure*, and (with Gail Watson) *Cooking Naturally For Pleasure and Health*, all published by Routledge & Kegan Paul.

How to Stop Smoking Easily

The Acugenic Method

Michael Blate
with Gail C. Watson, M.S.

London, Melbourne and Henley

First published in 1985
by ARKANA PAPERBACKS
ARKANA PAPERBACKS is an imprint of
Routledge & Kegan Paul plc
14 Leicester Square, London, WC2H 7PH, England

464 St Kilda Road, Melbourne,
Victoria 3004, Australia and

Broadway House, Newtown Road,
Henley-on-Thames, Oxon, RG9 1EN, England

Typeset by Columns, Reading
Printed and bound in Great Britain

ISBN 1-85063-008-9

For Laurie . . .

Contents

What is the G-Jo Institute?

The G-Jo Institute is a not-for-profit natural health research and educational organization. It was informally organized in 1976 and incorporated in 1982. Its purpose is the dissemination of drugless 'self-health' techniques.

G-Jo is a simplified form of acupuncture without needles (or 'acupressure'). However, the scope of the G-Jo Institute has expanded far beyond its original purpose of the sharing of simple acupressure techniques.

It is our belief that it is the body-mind – and *only* the body-mind – which heals itself. For that reason, we now address ourselves to the *entire* spectrum of how to stimulate the innate self-health in mechanisms within the body-mind using simple, yet effective, self-applied techniques from around the world.

For further information or catalogs about our publications, recordings, workshops and such, send a business-sized, self-addressed stamped envelope (or equivalent international postage stamps for locations outside the U.S.A.) to:

THE G-JO INSTITUTE
DIVISION SS
POST OFFICE BOX 8060-WL
HOLLYWOOD, FLA. 33084
U.S.A.

Acknowledgments

For all the information from teachers and authors about acupuncture and acupressure techniques, this author extends his sincerest appreciation. While many have contributed to the dissemination of information about these traditionally Oriental self-health methods, the reader is advised to see publications by the American authors: Dr. Ralph A. Dale (The Acupuncture Education Center, Miami, Florida); Dr. Pedro Chan (Center for Chinese Medicine, Monterey Park, California 91754); Dr. Robert E. Willner, M.D. (North Miami Beach, Florida 33165); Dr. John Thie, D.C. (Touch for Health Foundation, Pasadena, California); and numerous other popular author-teachers of these techniques.

In Great Britain, Dr. J.R. Worsley and Dr. Felix Mann have been at the forefront of acupuncture education, and the authors Denis and Joyce Lawson-Wood have provided the public with a great deal of useful self-health information. Their publications – as well as any other in the field of traditional Oriental self-applied health and healing techniques – are highly recommended.

What is ACUGENICS?

'Acugenics' means *that which has its basis in the acupuncture (energy) theory*. This traditionally-Oriental viewpoint believes that a vital force – called *bioenergy* – circulates from organ to organ throughout the body, making them produce the chemicals and electromagnetic impulses vital for life.

When bioenergy is moving smoothly from organ to organ – neither too quickly nor too slowly – we are in good health. But when any disruption or malfunction occurs within the energy system, symptoms appear and we are considered to be ill. In this Oriental point of view, there are thousands of symptoms but only one disease: an 'imbalanced' flow of bioenergy.

The techniques and information in the following pages have a single purpose – to help the body-mind restore balance and harmony within its bioenergy system. As this occurs, the 'target symptoms' – which in this case are the symptoms of addiction to tobacco – should 'reverse' (heal) themselves. As balance is restored in the energy system, the emotional or physical addiction drops away in response.

Foreword

Welcome to The G-Jo Institute Stop Smoking with Acugenics Program. Whether you are a smoker or simply a curious non-smoker, you will find useful, helpful information here. But let me begin by posing a couple of questions for you to ponder, and a bit of philosophy . . .

There is a way of approaching difficulties that promises the best possibility of learning and success. It begins with letting go of resistance and resentment. Can you look into the face of adversity and see there a hidden friend, ready to help you achieve your desires? Can you see there in your lit cigarette a cleansing fire that can be used to your advantage by burning away the weaknesses and imperfections that have limited you? It may be that your desire to give up your cigarette, cigar or pipe implies a readiness to live your entire life in a freer and more positive way.

I speak from experience. Like you, I have reviewed the facts: smoking is a major health risk. Statistically, it dramatically increases one's risk of death or disability from lung cancer, high blood pressure, and heart disease. It is also linked, through its effect on the digestive organs and the immune system, with hypoglycemia, arthritis, and other chronic health problems. It depletes the body's nutritional stores, adversely affects fertility and sex drive, and predisposes one to lung infections and emphysema. In short, it is SELF-POLLUTION, poisoning the body, clouding the mind, and impeding spiritual growth.

However, these 'scary' facts have in themselves done little to curb the smoking habit, at least in most of us. In the United States, though there has been a modest reduction in the average number of cigarettes smoked per capita (mainly because of increased cost of cigarettes), Americans still consume about half a pack of cigarettes per day, on the average. That statistic includes EVERY man and woman aged 18 and over, even the non-smokers, so that the smokers themselves consume many more.

One must conclude, then, that the pleasure of smoking (or at least, the transient feeling of well-being and tension relief that it brings) must be a POWERFUL force in favor of maintaining the habit. It begins to look a bit like a war between the 'good guys' (pleasurable feelings) and the 'bad guys' (scared feelings) as to who will ultimately win out. The bad news is that – in this old scenario – the 'bad guys' usually win ... and the smoking habit continues. The good news is that there IS a way to win. Ironically, it involves *giving up* the fight.

The book you are now holding is a strategy manual on how to give up smoking by giving up the FIGHT against it. No 'war on tobacco,' the author maintains; rather, the way out is to learn to love and enjoy it. Sound too easy? I urge you to try it. For me, it was only after I 'gave in' to my helplessness in 'winning' the battle of conflicting emotions that were raging within me that I was able to step OFF the battlefield and put my own cigarette smoking habit to rest ... and that was after 17 years!!

It might not be YOUR time right now to give up smoking forever, but it is an *ideal* time to look your addiction 'right in the butt' and see how you have let it control you and limit many of your other pleasures in life. Through making some modifications in your diet, increasing your level of exercise, and finding ways to improve your personal relationships you may bring yourself closer to the author's D-Day ('Drop' tobacco Day). And better yet, you may begin to discover an improved quality of life and pleasure that may 'hook' you into a delightful way of living that you had only dimly sensed.

So, here are the directions. You needn't STRUGGLE against tobacco (or even marijuana), or 'swim upstream' any longer. Make small commitments that you can keep and follow through on them. Breathe ease . . . and eventually, breathe smoke-free. From an ex-smoker, good luck!!

Barry Sultanoff, M.D.
Bethesda, Maryland

Introduction

Welcome to the G-Jo Institute *Stop Smoking with Acugenics (SSA) Program!* It is an unusual three-phase process that has proven itself extremely effective for stopping smoking – and 'staying stopped' – no matter how weak you now think you are when it comes to tobacco.

At this moment, you probably feel both frightened and skeptical, whether you realize it or not.

Frightened, because a deep-rooted part of you senses an important pleasure in your life is being threatened – and smoking *does* provide a pleasure that nearly nothing else can match.

Skeptical, because you've probably tried to stop before without much success (welcome to the 75% of smokers who have tried to become 'ex-smokers' – but haven't made it . . . yet).

Relax! The only thing you have to do right now is make a commitment to read this book. The next commitment – putting down your tobacco – will come only *after you're emotionally ready* to take that step – not before.

By then, you'll be well-armed with a full arsenal of tactics to get you over the humps. And if you decide you don't really want to stop smoking just yet, you'll have methods to insure that your smoking will do you less damage than it may be doing right now – even if you smoke as many cigarettes later as you're smoking today.

The reason for this is simple – the SSA Program teaches you to first *understand*, then truly *enjoy* (even *love*) your smoking. Then – and *only* then – do you allow yourself to release your addiction.

Meanwhile, the more you truly enjoy smoking, the less damage it will do to you.

This may seem strange, but think about it: your 'body-mind' has a complex protection system that rejects – often through disease or symptoms of disorder – any abuse you continually put to it. Smoking is obviously an abuse – you already know that or you wouldn't be reading this book.

But *pleasure* – the *true enjoyment* of any pastime (even smoking) – tends to override much of the body-mind's self-protective functioning. That is, at least for a long enough time for *all* your 'parts' – your *emotional* part as well as your intellectual part – to adjust to the idea that smoking really isn't much fun, and it's OK to let go and release it.

There are two important problems you suffer as a smoker. First, you have an emotional addiction to tobacco. And, second, you have a *physical* addiction, as well.

The SSA Program takes *both* parts of your addiction into consideration. And one day – perhaps very soon – you can look at the cigarette now clenched tightly between your fingers and see how truly *silly* the whole process of smoking really is.

This means having no hatred directed at yourself. Nor fear, either; and no guilt nor self-recriminations about how 'weak' you are – just a chuckle at your own silliness for being so attached to a process that neither tastes good, smells good nor has many real benefits – mostly drawbacks.

But you don't feel that way yet, or else you wouldn't

need this program, right? You've probably tried to stop smoking before by 'fighting it' – that is, whenever you felt the desire for a smoke, you had to exercise will power, or play little tricks on yourself like allowing yourself to only smoke one cigarette an hour . . . things like that. Most people who want to stop smoking give such tactics a try – *and they're about the worst things you can do if you really want to stop smoking!*

That's because such tactics keep you constantly thinking about smoking and they *reinforce your desire* to smoke. Where the mind leads, the action follows. In other words, *form follows thought*.

The handful of ex-smokers who actually 'fought the habit and beat it' usually become fanatics who are even less fun to be around now than they were while suffering from tobacco withdrawal. Have you met folks like that? If so, you probably don't want to become one of them.

Fighting is usually the least effective way to actually succeed at anything. It certainly isn't the best way to 'beat' your smoking addiction. By the way, do you recognize that you're addicted to tobacco in the truest sense of the word? Tobacco is one of the most addictive substances known to man – its use is accompanied by cravings, withdrawal symptoms and hunger, for it causes sufferers to take unreasonable actions.

That's because if you 'win,' you've probably suffered emotionally in the process (like spending many hours wishing for a smoke). And if you 'lose' – begin smoking, again, that is – you condemn yourself to the status of a 'loser,' making you feel badly about yourself and hating your lack of will-power or reinforcing a negative self-image.

No, with a 'win-or-lose' attitude, you're practically doomed to begin smoking again within a short time – and wishing you'd never stopped in the first place.

The SSA Program takes a different approach. Your

only requirement for this program to be effective is *you need to believe that smoking is harmful and that it would be good to quit as soon as you're comfortable with the idea*.

Since you're reading this book you're already halfway home. If you follow the three phases faithfully, the rest will fall painlessly into place. You move at your own speed, whenever it feels right for you. Stop smoking now or next year, it makes no difference.

It is better to stop *only* when you are both intellectually *and* emotionally prepared, for when that occurs, you will be quite free from withdrawal symptoms and temptations to return to smoking.

Phase I: Understanding and Coping with your Addiction

Step One: Understanding your Addiction

You probably recognize that you have a lag between your emotional willingness to stop smoking and the intellectual desire.

Your rational part – your intellect – has been overwhelmed with facts, figures and grim details about the perils of smoking. But your emotional part (the part of you that controls addictions) doesn't want to hear a word of it! If it *fully* accepted all the facts, you'd be able to immediately throw away your tobacco and never look back.

The main reason that you want to stop smoking – if you haven't had a severe health scare, anyway – is probably because your *intellect* has been nagging you, right?

Let's understand that vital *emotional* part – the part that's holding you back – a little better. If you think deeply about stopping smoking, you'll probably feel a curious sense of *fear* within you. It could be called a *fear of deprivation*. That is, a fear of being deprived of what may be your only pleasureful moments in the course of a long and tedious day.

Not surprisingly, your emotional part is *very* protective about letting go of that pleasure. We are all pleasure-seeking creatures at heart.

1

Your emotional part is what got you turned on to smoking when you were probably much younger — a child or teen-ager, perhaps. And there is *still* a piece of you that identifies your smoking with power, adulthood, sex ... all the 'good' things in life. Can you get in touch with that part now?

If you can't remember that special feeling, just ask yourself *why* you started smoking. Remember the coughing, headaches and nausea that you felt with the first pack or two? You really had to *work* to overcome your body's protective mechanisms that tried to stop you from abusing yourself. There must have been *some* powerful reasons for you to deliberately override the defense mechanisms of your body-and-mind (body-mind).

And there were! Power ... sex ... adulthood. ...

Try to recall now specifically why you began smoking — write down the most important reasons you can remember (example: because you wanted to impress Billy Smith or Mary Brown with how grown up and sexy you were — really be honest about it):

_____

_____

_____

_____

_____

_____

_____

Take more space if you need to, just be as honest as you can about why and whom you wanted to impress. (Note: for this program to be its most effective, you must actually *write* out these reasons, either here or on a separate piece of paper.)

Think about these reasons. Are they still important today? Do you feel better about yourself now, so that you don't have to keep up the image that smoking portrays?

And just what *does* the picture of someone smoking portray to you? Sexy? Tough? Write all of these things down, too. Try to be as specific as possible:

_____

_____

_____

_____

_____

_____

_____

_____

How do you compare to that image? Do you measure up? Are you as confident as your image of a smoker may be? As sexy and attractive? Do you need a cigarette to complete these images of yourself? Cigarette smoking – or pipe smoking for that matter, and cigars too – creates strong emotional crutches, as you may be well aware.

But smoking is as much a *physical* and physiological addiction as it is mental or emotional – perhaps even more so.

It's obvious to anyone who smokes that the *lungs* are strongly affected by tobacco smoking, especially if you inhale the smoke. (Note: the deeper you inhale smoke, the greater are its negative effects – if you're going to smoke, it's best to first fill your lungs at least halfway with air before taking a drag on your smoke; then you'll take less smoke in and get rid of more of its toxins when you exhale.)

Smokers who have become more enlightened are now

also aware that the *heart* is greatly affected by tobacco – smokers stand a three times higher risk of heart attacks than non-smokers.

And the *kidneys*, too, are very sensitive to tobacco smoke. Smokers have a much greater chance of suffering a stroke (which is strongly kidney-related) than non-smokers. At least in part, with both stroke and heart attacks, *carbon monoxide* appears to be a primary offensive factor, so you don't protect yourself by simply switching to low-tar-nicotine cigarettes.

But what very few Westerners realize is the role played by the *liver* (in combination with the *stomach*) in smoking addiction and tobacco-related diseases (this is really the key organ, in fact, since it is one of several digestive organs that 'controls' *addiction*).

However, Oriental doctors have known about the 'liver connection' for many years. Have you heard about all the successful *acupuncture* treatments for stopping smoking? That's what the acupuncturist is doing – treating the smoker's liver, stomach and other digestive organs to break the addiction to tobacco.

And, in a later part of this program, you, too, will learn powerful acu*PRESSURE* (acupuncture without needles) techniques to ease the transition and help your body-mind heal itself. They're very effective – especially when used in conjunction with the other methods in this program – and quite easy to apply.

These organs – the liver and stomach, which again are the key organs that control our addiction (to anything) – will be the primary 'targets' of this program. Let's discuss this for a moment.

If you're like most smokers, you could probably stop smoking easily right now . . . except for two important times – *following a meal* and *during or immediately after times of stressful activity or situations* (such as following sexual orgasm, etc.). Does that sound like you? Some people also need a smoke as soon as they awake or they literally can't get up.

The other times when you want to smoke – such as when the telephone rings or as a social barrier, to give you something to do with your hands, etc. – are more *emotional* addictions that can easily be broken with a little training and a few 'tricks.'

Those tricks, incidentally, might include: keeping cigarettes in one place, matches in another and the ashtray in a third (to make you stop and think before 'lighting up')... never keeping cigarettes near the phone... or any of the techniques you'll learn in the following pages.

But the two or three important times when you actually, *physically*, do *need* a cigarette are different conditions, entirely. That's true addiction, not just habit. And the liver and stomach are the organs most involved in this part of the smoking process.

What occurs when you smoke is a complex interaction of biochemicals that are triggered within your system as you light up. If you are an experienced smoker – that is, if you have smoked for several days or more – you have already crippled your digestive functions, possibly quite seriously (even if you don't recognize any of the symptoms).

The tobacco has especially 'stunned' the liver so it can no longer produce enough digestive biochemicals (again, in conjunction with the other organs of the digestive team) to properly perform digestion. That is, on their own – without the stimulus that tobacco provides – these digestive organs can no longer adequately maintain the process of *keeping your blood sugar at an adequate level at all times* (which is what digestion is actually all about). These organs are injured – they are ill and suffering.

As a smoker, your liver now needs a boost during

'peak loads' – such as the times when a full meal is sitting in your stomach or when adrenalin is running rampant in your bloodstream, for example. This is the key to understanding – then 'reversing' (healing) – your addiction.

Here's how the process works: the cigarette *forces* the beginning smoker's liver to produce *more* than it needs (tobacco is a liver stimulant). That's why headaches and nausea (both common symptoms of liver 'hyperactivity') are typical reactions in new smokers.

When it becomes apparent to the liver that the newly initiated smoker is going to continue abusing him- or herself (in spite of the warning reactions it has sent out), the liver surrenders to the abuse. In response, it now becomes sluggish, *underproducing* its chemicals in compensation for the boost that the substances in the tobacco are now regularly giving it. In short, the liver reacts to tobacco by becoming *hypoactive* (underactive).

Now the liver must depend on the tobacco for its 'fix' to work normally, especially when insulin and other digestive 'juices' are required (Note: Oriental philosophy says that while insulin is produced in other organs, the liver acts like a trigger or thermostat to control its flow.) So during extreme times of biochemical imbalance – most commonly after eating and in stressful situations – there *is* real, physical addiction.

This is why ex-smokers tend to crave sweets after a meal when they'd ordinarily turn to a cigarette. Sugar does essentially the same thing for the liver – gives it a fast boost in its biochemical production. This is also why some ex-smokers tend to put on weight after they stop smoking. The liver – which is also intimately involved in the weight-regulation process – is still sluggish in 'new' ex-smokers (those who have been stopped for less than three years, or so).

Therefore, ex-smokers tend to eat more to feel

'satisfied.' Or they reach for sweets frequently. Or both. (As an aside, eating sweets frequently is one of the key factors in much of the post-smoking depression and bouts of sudden anger that are such common symptoms of tobacco withdrawal – it is hypoglycemia or 'low blood sugar' that makes an ex-smoker an 'emotional yo-yo' until his digestive functions are returned more to normal.)

Understanding this process may be helpful in future days if it seems you explode emotionally for no reason, or are walking around in a foul or depressed mood, apparently for want of a cigarette. If you understand that you are actually suffering from hypoglycemia – low blood sugar – you can easily remedy the situation through a few, simple dietary tactics – *but eating sugar or other harsh sweets is not one of them!* That's actually one of the *worst* things you can eat in those circumstances. But we will discuss the better alternative tactics in Phase III.

Step Two: Enjoying your Addiction

It will come as no big surprise that many people who smoke don't actually enjoy their tobacco's taste, only the emotional support and 'energy boost' (or relaxation) that smoking brings.

There is a complex human mechanism called *homeostasis* that protects us from changing nearly anything in our lives too quickly. This protection from abrupt change even stops us from changing self-destructive practices (such as smoking) too quickly, once we have incorporated them into our lives. Why and how this mechanism works is unimportant – but there is no doubt we must contend with it when letting tobacco drop from our lives.

Once we learn something – even if it is a wrong or

7

harmful something – we can't just 'unlearn' it. For example: have you ever had a relationship with a person that you knew was wrong for you, yet you couldn't let that person go? Or have you ever had a hobby that was a bit dangerous – riding a motorcycle, for instance – that you couldn't comfortably release in spite of the known dangers? Your *emotional* addiction to smoking is one of those kinds of activities.

What we *can* do is learn new data or techniques to 'override' our 'old' learned behavior – and that's how this SSA Program works. While your physical addiction to smoking requires different tactics (and you'll learn some amazingly effective ones), the fastest – and possibly the only *real* – way to break your emotional addiction to smoking is to learn to *love and enjoy it!*

Does this sound strange? Why should you deliberately set about trying to enjoy something you *know* isn't good for you? Well, why *shouldn't* you? After all, you're already addicted to smoking, even when you know it's probably doing you some harm. Knowing all the dire facts hasn't really impressed you enough to force you to quit – only created conflict within you.

So if you do nothing more than ease that conflict and get back to the 'good old days' when smoking seemed to please you, you've accomplished a great deal. If you're going to take all those risks, at least you should get some of the benefits, too. And there *are* benefits from smoking, not just risks. For example, smokers are six times less likely to develop dangerous ulcerative colitis than non-smokers (smoking acts to 'defuse' the harsh emotions that are thought to lead to colitis).

Furthermore, the body-mind is a marvelous, *self-healing* mechanism. It constantly tries to heal itself and will do a heroic job of it, as long as it isn't in terrible shape already. So you probably have some lead time before you need to make any hard commitments to release tobacco from your life, especially if you seem to be in pretty good health.

Here are some facts about smoking and smokers which should be encouraging (you've probably heard enough *discouraging* news about smoking to last you a lifetime already):

The most damaging influences to the body-mind from smoking appear to arise within the *immunological system* – the one that is involved with warding off allergic (and similar) reactions. It is a very easily healed part of the system. Generally, healing occurs simply by dropping the allergenic substance from your life. And since most people suffer from 'hidden allergies' to all tobacco products (tobacco is a member of the deadly nightshade family of plants), there is little doubt that the immunological system is very much involved in the disease aspect of smoking addiction;

While it takes several years – actually five to ten years – to really 'clean up' an ex-smoker's entire system and restore it to that comparable state of a non-smoker, the benefits of stopping smoking begin immediately – it's never too late to stop!

The risk for heart attack is cut by one half within the first six months after you stop smoking;

There are a number of herbal 'smokes' which – while they don't have exactly the same 'kick' as a cigarette – can actually be *beneficial* for you! You'll learn which they are in a few pages.

Now that you understand some of the dynamics of smoking, it's a great time to move on to the fun part – learning to *love* your cigarette!

Before going any further, please memorize this immutable law of human nature: YOU CAN'T RELEASE WHAT YOU DON'T LOVE (because you have too many unresolved feelings about it ... call it 'unfinished business')! Paste it up on a wall.

This includes ALL addictions – alcohol ... food ... relationships with 'unhealthy' people in your life – but most especially this is true about smoking. Unless and until you love your smoke, it is going to 'haunt' you whenever times get tough and you need some comfort. This natural law – that you can't conclude what you don't love – is a small portion of what the Orientals call 'the law of karma.'

So how do you learn to love your cigarette? Pay attention to it! Lavish it with all the honor it deserves as a pleasureful force in your life! It may be one of the few real or imagined pleasures (is there actually any difference?) you now have, so it's certainly due that honor.

And, specifically, *how* should you honor that pleasure? There are several steps (and you must follow them exactly to make this program work its fastest for you).

1. *Roll your own cigarettes ...* buy a 'custom blend' of tobacco if you live near a tobacco shop. There, you can usually find all the material you need for 'rolling your own' – a machine, paper, filters (if you like them), and, of course, good tobacco. If there's no such shop near you, many neighborhood convenience stores or 'head shops' now have all you'll need to get started. Or you might be able to get them by mail. Not only will you create much better tasting cigarettes, but you'll also save a bundle of money on your smokes. However, for this technique to be an effective way of bringing you pleasure in smoking, *you must roll only one cigarette at a time – and only when you're ready to*

smoke it! If you want this technique to work, rolling your cigarette must become a celebration and a ceremony to honor the pleasure you are about to receive. It is a cherished moment in your day – *honor it!*

2. *When you smoke . . . smoke.* Don't do *anything* else. Stop. Sit down. Relax. Roll your cigarette. Pay attention to what you are doing. Look at the product you've just manufactured. Light up . . . and enjoy! If you don't have the time to spend the 10 or 15 minutes enjoying your smoke, don't smoke until you can. (Incidentally, rolling cigarettes is very easy using a machine – it should only take a couple of cigarettes to perfect your skill.) Try to think of nothing else when you smoke except the pleasure you're receiving . . . taste your smoke – really get involved with it. If you have difficulty thinking only about smoking, try to make sure you think only pleasureful thoughts about other things.

3. *When you sense you've had enough – or when the smoke doesn't taste good anymore* (usually after the first few puffs) *put the cigarette out.* Throw it away. Don't save it for later, even though it may offend your sense of economy and thriftiness – after all, you're already saving a lot of money by rolling your own. To save the rest of the cigarette until later – when you're supposed to roll a new one – is really defeating the purpose. Besides, it will taste terrible and won't bring you pleasure.

4. *Smoke as many cigarettes a day as you want, but always follow the same steps* – relax . . . create your cigarette . . . smoke and enjoy . . . discard as soon as you feel satisfied. Don't take extra 'puffs' just to be thrifty – or, if you find yourself wanting to smoke your cigarette down to a nub, at least see if you can sense a fear within you that 'unless you get your

pleasure right now, you might not get it at all' (fear of deprivation).

Do these steps sound too complicated to you? Remember: it's fear of being deprived of pleasure that goads us into 'getting it now' (even if we don't really want it, or need it just now), and it's important to get past that point as quickly as you can. Just becoming aware that you *are* afraid of being deprived of your pleasure – then seeing how foolish it is, because you have allowed yourself the right to smoke *any time and as often as you want to* – will carry you easily over that major stumbling block.

(Note: the same *principles* – loving your smoke before you can release it – operate for pipe- and cigar-smokers, as well; but obviously this *technique* of 'rolling your own' will not apply . . . do use the rest of the methods in this program, however.)

Step Three: Prayer

We all have a gut understanding of prayer – asking God or some Higher Force within or outside of us for help when we don't seem to have answers ourselves – and most of us sense that there is a 'rightness' to praying. It is one common trait that we human beings seem to have – the desire and ability to pray. Yet surprisingly few people actually *exercise* this powerful self-health tactic for their most obvious needs.

For example, very few people even *think* about praying for help in their efforts to release their tobacco addiction. It's almost as if they feel *ashamed* to ask for help, or that it seems foolish or weak to ask for Divine Intervention for something as 'petty' as tobacco addiction. But prayer is going to be an important tool for you to use in learning to love your tobacco, your addiction . . . and yourself.

Whether prayer actually reaches the hidden ears of a Higher Force or taps a well-spring of hidden strength *within* us – or both (or more) – makes no difference. The most important thing is that *somehow prayer works!* Especially when it is combined with personal commitment.

Understand this: even if you now think you don't really want to stop smoking (and you're only reading this book as a favor to your doctor, a friend or a family member), if you simply begin praying for help in reaching that stubborn part of you – the self-destructive emotional part that refuses to 'see the light' and is afraid to even *want* to release the addiction – eventually something within you *will* get the message. You don't have to do anything else (besides *understanding* and *enjoying*, of course) – just pray. Eventually the process takes effect . . . almost in spite of you!

There are two vital aspects for a prayer to be its most effective:

> You must *acknowledge* that you are having a problem – in this case, an addiction to smoking that is hard (seemingly impossible, perhaps) to release by yourself . . .

> You must *request help* from *wherever* it comes . . . and be open to receiving this help, from whatever its source.

But remember the rule that *you can't fully release anything that you don't love*. When you pray – for prayer to be its most loving (and thus most effective) – don't talk about your smoking addiction as if it were some devilish malignancy of your soul, or some accursed parasite that is clinging to you. Instead, see it as your ignorance – or, if you prefer, your illness. Or maybe even a friend who has now overstayed his welcome. Nothing more – not a *moral* issue, especially. (Do you get the picture? You're only praying about *you* – and your lungs and liver and other digestive organs which you have injured – nothing else.)

Pray with lots of love for yourself, not hatred nor self-contempt. Of all three preparatory steps of the SSA Program, prayer can be by far the most effective – when properly done.

What is a 'proper prayer?' A good, basic prayer might go something like this: *'dear God (or Cosmic Spirit or Higher Self, etc.) . . . I have a hunger for smoking tobacco that is hard for me to release on my own . . . please help me to love, enjoy and release this hunger in the most pleasant and painless way You see fit.'*

This prayer is best done before rolling each cigarette. In fact, you could even add to your prayer – if you make the prayer a practice while fixing your cigarette – *' . . . please accept this gift of my love for You, dear God, and know that I am thinking of You as I enjoy this smoke.'*

If this seems somehow 'sinful' – as it may to people who have very strict or fundamental backgrounds – please remember that many cultures have actually *used* tobacco or other smokables as a 'true path' – you might call them 'sacraments' – to finding God.

Spiritually, it is quite possible that smoking is not a sinful practice, only that it slows enlightenment by keeping one attached to an unhealthy addiction. It is also written in most spiritual texts that God loves everything and everybody. He created everything in this world for His purpose. And His biggest pleasure – if this author's interpretation of the world's major spiritual writings is correct – is for people to pay devout attention and devotion to Him (or Her or It).

These three steps – understanding . . . love and enjoyment . . . prayer – will soon allow you to release tobacco addiction from your life. If you follow these steps faithfully, your tobacco addiction *must* drop away – it cannot fail to occur!

Phase II: D-Day – And its Preparation

A day will come when you will actually *see* (not just intellectually, but in all parts of your being) the silliness of the cigarette, cigar or pipe you now so desperately cling to – assuming you have followed the steps previously described. On that day, your rational, thinking part will say 'sure, why not now? It's OK with me to *try* letting go. I think I can do it!' That day – we'll call it *D-Day* (for Drop Day) – will mark a new step towards freedom and health in your life.

There is every possibility that at that moment you will drop tobacco without serious withdrawal symptoms (more about these later) – especially if you have already begun applying the following techniques before D-Day arrives.

Before discussing those, let's talk about D-Day for a moment. It will be a big and possibly frightening experience for you to let your cigarette 'fixin's' (or other smokes) drop into the waste basket. But that's where they must *immediately* go – out! You must go 'cold turkey' on D-Day for the SSA Program to be effective for you.

However, *you always keep your options open-ended.* You make no commitment to stop smoking forever – only for as long as you think you can stop without feeling threatened and frantic.

If it's one day, fine. If it's a week, better. Whatever

you think you can handle, commit yourself *only* for that long – no longer!

Give yourself permission to go back to smoking *any* time after you finish your commitment – all it takes is going back to your tobacconist's for another batch of inexpensive fixin's. (OK – if you've found a particularly 'simpatico' rolling machine, keep it, if it makes you feel more secure – that way, all you'll need are tobacco and papers, both of which can be had at a moment's notice in most convenience stores. The same for your favorite pipes – keep them, if it helps. Or if you have a box of prime Cuban cigars, store them in a friend's freezer, if throwing them out hurts too much.)

If you decide to return to smoking after your commitment time has expired, simply follow the pre-D-Day rules – understand . . . love and enjoy . . . pray. While you may have been a little premature, you're definitely *not a failure* if you decide to return to smoking for a while longer.

Maybe tomorrow will be another good time . . . or next week – whatever feels right. Until then, as the old *Zen* saying goes: *don't push the river*. Just relax and enjoy!

But think of going back to smoking as a *last* resort – something to do *after* you've exhausted the following 'arsenal' of self-help and 'first-aid' methods to help you past the potentially difficult times of withdrawal. These tactics are designed to ease both the emotional and physical addiction that tobacco has caused. They should be followed carefully for their full effectiveness to be felt.

As mentioned earlier, the following 'self-health' tactics are actually best begun *now*, in conjunction with the beginning of your three-step SSA Program.

The first tactic is to *start keeping a daily journal or diary*. Part of the reason that you are emotionally addicted to smoking is because smoking is a good way of venting aggressive and hostile feelings – unfortunately

17

upon yourself. You can consider it an ideal method for 'burning' the harsh words you might otherwise have wished to say. (Anger, incidentally, is another function that is 'controlled' by the liver, according to Oriental acupuncturists.)

At the root of all anger is *fear*. Not only will your writing help vent unspoken words, but it may even reveal the depth and source of the fear(s) behind it. This is a *very* powerful technique.

It is *essential* to have a way of expressing those words and feelings that used to be 'burned up in smoke.' A simple diary will do, noting any observations you can make about yourself, your anger and fears – even your pleasures – which you encounter on a day-to-day basis. This is a hard concept to fully appreciate – that is, that smoking is a useful 'substitute' for aggressive, hostile feelings – and it pays to think about it well.

You may see for yourself that the only things keeping you addicted to your tobacco are fear, guilt and self-recrimination – not pleasure, at all. Please allow yourself to understand that it's OK for you to feel that way – just try to be detached . . . try to stand back and see the emotional hoops you force yourself to jump through as soon as you threaten yourself with even the *idea* of stopping smoking.

Another important step you *must* do for this program to proceed along its normal path is *deep breathing for at least ten complete cycles twice a day*.

The only time that many smokers breathe more than very shallowly is when they are smoking their cigarettes. Part of the 'addiction' is really nothing more than a craving by the lungs for expansion and more air!

To do this exercise, empty all the air from your lungs, then breathe in through your nostrils slowly, deeply, beginning from your lower abdomen. Then breathe 'all the way up' to the 'top' of your lungs, expanding them as much as possible.

Hold that breath for a few moments – say, for a count of four or five – then exhale the same way, slowly through the nose, finally forcing all the air from your lungs by compressing your lower abdomen. Repeat this process ten times or more during each of your twice-daily sessions.

You can even make your deep breathing a *cleansing* process, if you'll exhale your breath through pursed lips (rather than the nostrils), exhaling as hard as you can against your pursed lips to 'exercise' the lungs and chest areas.

An even more effective – if somewhat silly looking – cleansing breath technique is the 'lion pose' taught by many *yogis*. Here, you kneel on the floor, hands placed upon your knees. Then inhale and, *with the mouth and eyes open as wide as possible, stick your tongue out as far as it will go and exhale sharply and completely with a loudly 'whispered' HAAAAH*!

Repeating this several times is also an excellent way to relieve (or even cure) a sore throat! It really works!

Any deep-breathing technique is also a good 'first-aid' method for when you want to smoke, but can't because you don't have the time to fully enjoy it (or if you feel a 'nicotine fit' coming on). Just breathe deeply . . . within moments, your desire for a smoke will pass. Many smokers have been 'cured' by deep breathing, alone.

Because of their effects on certain organs – most notably, but not restricted to, the digestive organs – there are certain foods which are best avoided as much as possible if you want to make stopping smoking as painless as possible. Some of these foods are:

meat and all slaughtered animal products – these create a 'heaviness' within the digestive tract that requires an enormous processing effort by the liver and other organs. Sugar, alcohol – or, of course, tobacco – will be yearned for to give the liver its extra boost . . .

eggs . . .

salt (other than small amounts used in cooking) . . .

SUGAR – it creates a vicious cycle (called the low blood-sugar of hypoglycemic reaction) which causes you to become an 'emotional yo-yo.' Remember: *this includes all sugary foods and drinks*! Even honey or other harshly sweet substances should be aovided – they have nearly identical effects!

alcohol in excess (more than one small drink a day), because alcohol has the same effect as sugar – except more intense – and it also often triggers a hunger for a smoke . . .

refined carbohydrates (e.g.: white bread, pasta, many processed foods, etc.) *and caffeinated drinks* (especially coffee) – again, the same effect, but not usually as drastic, as with sugar or alcohol . . .

'recreational' or excessive *medicinal drugs* – they, too, have a harsh effect on the liver . . .

heavy meals – they create too much of a strain on the liver (thus requiring more of a 'boost') . . . a better idea is to eat lighter meals, but more frequently than the usual 'three squares a day.' This is also good therapy for anyone suffering from hypoglycemia (which probably includes most smokers). Select from the recipes in the final section of this manual. As a very wise general practice, always eat your heavier meals *early* in the day – not later (especially after dark). The digestive organs are most active – and thus require less stimulation – from early morning until early afternoon.

All diseases – including tobacco addiction – create certain nutritional deficiencies. When you 'counter' these deficiencies by temporarily adding various 'medicinal' foods and supplements to your diet, you'll find that your smoking hunger is greatly reduced.

In fact, with proper nutrition, you may actually find

20

yourself getting nauseous when you first light up a
smoke – just like those 'good old' youthful days when you
first began smoking.

Medicinal foods for smokers – that is, those foods
which nourish and stimulate the afflicted organs to
produce more of the vital biochemicals than they are
presently producing – include (in moderation) *unsalted
peanuts* (preferably boiled), *soybeans (and soybean products), Brazil nuts, cashews, sesame seeds, sunflower seeds
and brewer's yeast.* (Note: recent information, however,
indicates that many people have a 'hidden allergy' to
brewer's yeast – which has been one of the 'miracle
foods' of the health food industry – so use this substance
cautiously.) *Fresh fruits and vegetables* – especially in
the form of freshly-squeezed or blended juices – are also
highly recommended.

A most important food for ex-smokers (and hypoglycemic people) is the *Jerusalem artichoke,* which is
now available in many supermarkets. This food – which
looks rather like a ginger root but tastes like the heart
of an artichoke – helps control the normal craving for
sweets that most smokers suffer in the first few weeks of
becoming ex-smokers.

Of the various supplements – all of which are
available from your local health food store, but which
shouldn't be taken for more than six months or so (since
you may easily create another addiction, this time to
vitamins) – include the following:

vitamin B complex;
vitamin A;
vitamin C;
vitamin E;
niacinamide (use this cautiously);
thiamine (also use this cautiously);
pyridoxine;

zinc;
selenium;
cysteine (an amino acid);
fructose (use this *in moderation* instead of sugar).

There are a number of important non-nutritional needs an ex-smoker has, just like anyone else in the world. Only an ex-smoker needs them more – if he wants to *stay* an ex-smoker.

Physical exercise is extremely important, especially just after D-Day. Here again, the reason is the liver. Nothing stimulates the liver into proper activity like exercise or physical movement (the liver is closely related to the body's muscles – stimulating the muscles also stimulates the liver).

Even 3 or 4 minutes' worth of moderate exercise is usually enough – something like a slow, gentle, free-form *dance*, or *walking* 300-400 steps – even just a good stretch – these, and other gentle activities will quickly reduce both the emotional and especially the physical craving for a smoke.

And while *running* has many drawbacks as a healthful activity, jogging or 'fast walking' may help you past the psychological concern that you're not really doing enough to help yourself restore health simply by doing a few minutes of easy movement.

It's good practice for ex-smokers to reach out for *emotional support* from an understanding person or group. The emotional parts of smoking are deep and complex; many smokers have a sense of being 'worthless losers' or they harbor self-destructive feelings. They *need* to fail to be comfortable, and the threat of being successful at stopping smoking (or with *any* kind of success, for that matter) presents some big difficulties. Here, emotional support is very important. And in some cases, even professional (psychotherapeutic) help is needed.

There are numerous church groups, YMCAs and other socio-religious organizations that run stop-smoking programs. These are often good resources for that kind of support, at least in the beginning. Later, you won't need it. But beware of any group that would label smoking a 'sin' – it is an illness, nothing more (and nothing less).

There are also stop-smoking clinics – but their programs may cost upwards of several hundred dollars (in America), and these organizations usually have their own methods and formats for stopping smoking which you are expected to follow.

In any event, linking hands with others who are dropping tobacco addiction is a good way to find emotional support and to meet new people, as well. If there are 'growth centers' in your community, they may be good resources for such support, too.

However, bars, pubs and nightclubs offer *negative support*, and if you're serious about stopping smoking, it's best to avoid such places – at least until you're a comfortable ex-smoker.

Let's review where we now stand for a moment. As quickly as possible you should begin: adding certain foods and supplements . . . avoiding certain 'triggering' foods (like meat, alcohol or coffee) . . . doing deep breathing regularly . . . rolling your own cigarettes and taking time to enjoy them properly . . . keeping a brief, daily journal of your adventure into self-discovery through the process of becoming an ex-smoker . . . praying, of course – and very soon, D-Day!

When D-Day happens, remember: *don't make a big commitment* – set a small goal for yourself. Go for one or two days without smoking. See how it feels. Or try a week. But don't commit yourself to stop smoking 'forever,' because you may be setting yourself up for a relapse within even a few hours! And give yourself permission to back out of your commitment with grace if the going gets too tough.

Remember, also: *go cold turkey!* When you stop – stop. Don't try tapering off, because the statistics are dead-set against you. If the idea of stopping cold for two days is too heavy, stop for one. Or even an hour. But do it flat. No compromises. Just keep adding new commitments as you go.

Your first few days of ex-smoking may bring about some withdrawal symptoms that you'll want to be aware of. Some of the most common are *hyperactivity, drowsiness and tiredness, dizziness, short-temperedness, nausea, memory loss or difficulties* (these are mostly liver-related symptoms), plus *anxiousness – even harsh fear or terror – irrationality, or changes in breathing patterns*.

For many people in the SSA Program, a day or two of these withdrawal symptoms are all that will be suffered and the need to smoke will never bother them again – at least, not enough to suffer a relapse. (Even here, there are techniques, you'll learn in a moment to *dramatically* ease those unpleasant reactions.) These are ex-smokers who have truly learned to love their cigarettes.

And, through that love and self-acceptance, these ex-smokers have discovered emotionally that smoking had mostly unredeeming qualities. Bad taste . . . foul smell . . . unpleasant and unhealthy reactions within their systems – these ex-smokers have learned to *fully* accept what most smokers at least know intellectually: smoking addiction holds nothing more of value for a healthy, happy person.

But in the event you aren't so fortunate as to be able to go cold turkey without uncomfortable withdrawal symptoms, there are certain precautions you should take before you make any commitment to D-Day.

One most important precaution is to stock up on a number of smoking and drinking herbs that may be nothing short of miraculous in helping you through this withdrawal period. You can find the following herbs in most health food stores (you don't have to get all of them – just a few of them will do, but at least try to get those which are underlined).

If there are no health food stores near you, herbs are easily available by mail – check such publications as *Organic Gardening or Prevention Magazine* (in America, or in various natural health publications elsewhere), or try local gardening publications for those sources.

The herbs you'll want to purchase include the following (with the most important ones underlined):

<u>mullein</u>
<u>licorice root</u>
<u>comfrey</u>
dittany
lobelia
eyebright
thyme
damiana
deer tongue
hyssop
buckbean
cornsilk
sage
spearmint
betony
chamomile
red clover
motherwort
coltsfoot
cubeb berries
yerba santa
cinnamon sticks
rosemary

lavender
strawberry leaves

If possible, you'll also want a water pipe or *hookah*. This is the most 'healthy' way to smoke anything – with the smoke being filtered and cooled through water, wine or fruit juice. While this may be a bit exotic for some people's tastes, if your health and your smoking habit are on a collision course, the water pipe may well be a most useful temporary alternative. And it's perfect for smoking herbs and herbal blends.

While most of these herbs can be brewed into teas or infusions, mullein, comfrey or several other herbs on this list can easily be rolled into 'cigarettes,' and the water pipe (available in any 'head shop' or by mail through most youth-oriented magazines) is, as mentioned, an even better way to smoke them.

Mullein, especially, is good to smoke on an occasional basis (say, three cigarettes or one small bowlful daily, for a few weeks), and many of the other herbs can be blended into a water pipe mixture that is both cool and even beneficial – *in moderation*. Several suggested combinations (mixed in approximately equal proportions, or to taste) are:

* buckbean, eyebright, betony, rosemary, thyme, lavender and chamomile
* damiana, red clover and strawberry leaves
* deer tongue, damiana, yerba santa, lobelia, coltsfoot and motherwort
* spearmint, damiana, coltsfoot and hyssop
* mullein, cubeb berries, lobelia and mint.

These herbal 'smokes' should be the heart of your 'ex-smoker's survival kit.' You may never need them, but if times start getting tough for you, try these first before going back to tobacco. You may find they satisfy much of the need – along with the deep breathing exercises you should be continuing on a daily basis – to get you past most of your withdrawal crises.

One of the ex-smoker's best herbal friends is *licorice*, in twig or branch form. When you feel a desire for a cigarette, instead chew on a piece of licorice twig for a few minutes – the results are usually nothing short of miraculous! But please note: *use real licorice twigs – not licorice-flavored candy or 'twists.'* These twigs should be readily available in many health food stores, like most of the other herbs.

An interesting, if rather spicy alternative to curb the desire for a cigarette is to *chew a hot pepper* whenever the urge strikes! It works rather quickly (within a week, or so, according to first-hand reports) . . . but it may be a slightly painful way of killling the desire for tobacco.

Yet this is not just a psychological ploy to help associate the desire for tobacco with a painful sensation. Both the peppers and tobacco are members of the nightshade family of plants, and so there are several common elements to both these substances. And both affect the lungs.

It is important to continue your diary or journal on a regular, daily basis from D-Day forward. This is one of the most helpful aids you can give yourself, because nothing assists self-discovery more than verbalizing or writing your thoughts and feelings.

These insights become particularly important several days, weeks or even months later. The nature of the human mind is often to forget our particularly important insights and self-revelations within a short time. Reviewing your diary occasionally will help you easily recall these important observations . . . and help you reinforce your commitment to be well.

The goal of such 'self-psychotherapy' is to release harsh feelings, either through spoken or written words, but not through destructive activities (like smoking) and not by stashing and storing them (or even just speaking them silently in your mind). For many smokers, it is a natural habit to reach for a smoke when they are angry and give themselves some pain in the lungs, rather than verbalizing their angers and frustrations.

Try to get past this point with yourself, for it is a self-destructive trait and one that could easily lead you right back to smoking (or toward other self-destructive activities) if you don't have some real and useful alternatives – like a diary – for dealing with your own, strong feelings.

There is one more vital tactic for self-health and helping you past the crisis point in your SSA Program. This is called *G-Jo* – a simplified form of acupuncture without needles (finger-pressure acupuncture, or 'acupressure').

This ancient, Oriental technique is an important part of this program and provides almost immediate relief from many of the withdrawal symptoms associated with tobacco addiction (when used in conjunction with the other SSA tactics). This is especially true for easing the hunger for excess foods and sweets, and to curb the desire for tobacco.

The reason the following techniques work is because when you use G-Jo for symptomatic relief from tobacco addiction, you are actually stimulating your liver and other digestive organs, as well as your lungs and heart. Using G-Jo, you are, in effect, manually 'forcing' your organs to create the necessary biochemicals to provide you a sense of satisfaction. When this occurs, those withdrawal symptoms are promptly relieved.

There are 116 G-Jo acupressure points to relieve more than 250 symptoms and health problems of all kinds, tobacco addiction being just one of them. (All the G-Jo techniques can be found in *The Natural Healer's*

Acupressure Handbook, Volume I: Basic G-Jo, by this author, and available in Great Britain through Routledge & Kegan Paul, Ltd. – see address at the front of this book.)

G-Jo is a most useful tool if you enjoy freedom from doctors and drugs, and if you like the idea of being able to relieve most health disorders with nothing more than the touch of a finger.

While there are a number of G-Jo smoking relief points, perhaps only two or three will work particularly well for you. Each person is different, each has different organ imbalances caused by his or her smoking.

So it is suggested that you try all the points in the beginning of this program, then focus on those which are either the most tender or seem to bring the most relief during 'acute' times or moments of stress. If you use G-Jo properly, there will be no doubt that you are getting relief using this technique. And it should happen *immediately*.

For smokers' symptoms, relief will often come in the form of a profound sense of relaxation. The 'hunger' for tobacco causes a feeling of stress and tension within – the acupressure (when properly applied) produces an immediate feeling of relief . . . in the form of relaxation. And it will often help reduce the hunger for tobacco, too, so that the cravings occur less and less frequently.

There are two important rules for using G-Jo. You must *first find the right G-Jo point; then you must stimulate that point properly*.

To find the G-Jo point, probe the corresponding area on your own body (see following illustrations for reference) *as deeply as you can* (using up to 20 lbs of pressure). You're looking for a tender 'ouch spot' – a sensitive spot in that area which feels distinctly different from the surrounding flesh.

It may feel like a toothache or announce itself with a

twinge of pain like a pinched nerve when you probe the spot deeply. You must feel that 'ouch,' though, or you haven't found the point . . . keep probing until you do. Since the points are only about the size of a pinhead, you'll have to search carefully.

Once you locate the point, deeply massage it with a digging, goading kind of fingertip stimulation or massage. You only need to do this for a few seconds – 15 or 20 seconds at the most – and you should feel that sense of immediate relief.

Most of these points are duplicated bilaterally (on either side of the body) so you should stimulate both sides equally (except when the points are in vertical line with the navel – then there are no duplicated points). If discomfort returns, restimulate – but not over five or six times daily, as a general practice.

These points are actually 'triggered' only until you feel an 'acupressure reaction' – that is, a feeling of warmth, clamminess, perspiration or such. This reaction tells you you've found – and triggered – a good G-Jo point properly. For acupressure points in the ear, use a wooden matchstick or a blunt toothpick to both find, then trigger – but use *gentle* pressure . . . ear points can be surprisingly tender.

While G-Jo is a safe and harmless technique, there are several contraindications or times when G-Jo should be avoided. You should not use G-Jo if:

* You are a pregnant women, especially beyond the third month of pregnancy;
* You are a chronic heart patient, especially if you wear a pacemaker or similar energy-regulating device;
* You take regular or daily medication for serious health problems (e.g. cancer, diabetes, etc.).

General Acupressure Points

Throat Point

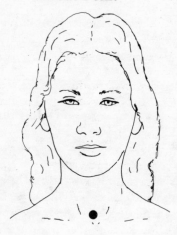

G-Jo Point 1

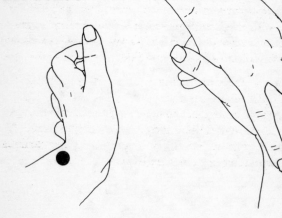

G-Jo Point 7

G-Jo Point 9

G-Jo Point 10

G-Jo Point 11

G-Jo Point 17

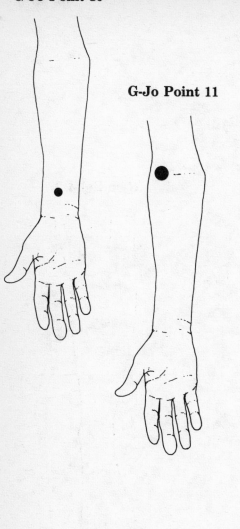

G-Jo Point 31

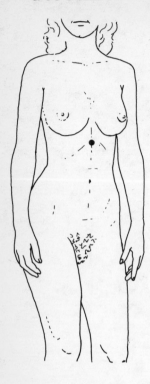

G-Jo Point 97

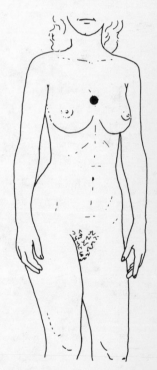

G-Jo Point 115

G-Jo Ear Points

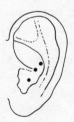

Phase III: Recipes for Ex-Smokers

Because the liver and digestive organs are actually crippled in smokers and new ex-smokers, these organs are more sluggish and less quick to respond to the 'appestat' controls that the body depends upon to regulate appetite, hunger and satiation. For this reason, ex-smokers tend to eat more food and, hence, put on weight rather easily. The following snacks will be particularly helpful (as an alternative to harsh sweets) for raising blood sugar levels during periods of stress or hunger that happen 'too early' before the next meal.

The following recipes have been selected in part from the G-Jo Institute's natural foods cooking and teaching book, COOKING NATURALLY FOR PLEASURE AND HEALTH (published in the U.K. by this publisher). They serve at least two purposes. First, to stimulate the liver and provide fast hunger relief *without* being overly fattening. And, second, to present healthful, 'low-fattening' foods in tasty and attractive ways. These recipes are entirely vegetarian and may be pleasurefully consumed by people of all faiths and philosophies.

Not only are they healthful, but they're quite delicious, too. Each of them has been 'taste-tested' many times at our teaching and research facilities in Florida. They are favorites in the classes that we hold regularly at the Institute.

There is a 'basic' diet – based on the lacto-vegetarian

way of eating (a vegetarian diet that includes rennetless dairy products) – which may be used by virtually everyone without fear of nutritional deficiency. It may be adjusted downwards (for weight loss) or upwards (to maintain or increase weight) as necessary, and has essentially been approved by most leading Western health agencies (including The American Medical Association).

This diet is based on a 'numbers-of-servings-per-day' arrangement. There are four basic groups:

* The milk group – include at least *two* servings each day of the following foods: one cup of whole, low-fat or skim milk; one cup of buttermilk; one cup of low-fat yogurt; one cup of dry or low-fat cottage cheese; two slices of (preferably rennetless) cheese. (Note: when dairy allergy exists, 'milk' from seeds or nuts may be substituted – see recipes below);
* The protein group – include at least *two* servings daily of the following foods: one cup cooked dried beans; one cup cooked dried peas; one cup cooked dried lentils; one-half to three-quarters cup of (unsalted) nuts or peanuts; one cup of cooked soybeans or soybean products (e.g. tofu, bean curd, tempeh, etc.); (optional, but not recommended – two eggs);
* The grain/cereal group – include at least *four* servings daily of the following foods (selecting whole grain or unrefined products, whenever possible): one slice of bread; one roll, bun or muffin; one-half to three-quarters cup cooked or ready-to-eat cereal or grain, rice or pasta (macaroni, noodles, spaghetti);
* The fruit/vegetable group – include at least *four* servings daily of any fresh fruit or vegetable (in moderate amounts), which may be taken either in whole or juice form.

These foods should be consumed in five or six smaller

meals throughout the day, rather than two or three larger meals – especially if weight loss or maintenance is the goal. Largest meals should be consumed earlier in the day with only light snacking of healthful foods (from the above groups) occurring later in the day or evening.

This diet will generally provide enough vitamins, minerals, calories and other nutritional requirements for a person leading a moderately-active to active lifestyle. For the average person trying to lose weight, 1200 to 1600 calories a day from the above food selections should provide a gradual and sustainable weight loss. Over 1600 calories a day will generally either maintain or increase weight, depending on one's job, stress level, etc.

It is wise, however, to reduce – then eliminate – all dairy products (milk, cheese, etc.) as quickly as possible. These foods are a major source of 'hidden' allergic reactions. Their primary benefit is simply to provide a good source of vitamin B_{12} for 'beginning' vegetarians.

If you need an effective weight loss program, see this author's HOW TO LOSE WEIGHT EASILY: THE ACUGENIC METHOD (published in the U.K. by the same publishers). And an effective fitness program for people of all ages, also based on the Acugenics concept, is described in HOW TO GET FIT – AND STAY FIT: THE ACUGENIC METHOD (by the same author, also published in the U.K. by this publisher).

Eating naturally for pleasure and health is a grand adventure. Pursue it joyfully with love and peace in your heart.

Recipe Index

Peanut Butter Cookies, p. 72
Raisin-Spice Cookies, p. 72
Sesame Candy, p. 73
Sesame Halvah, p. 73
Sunflower Seed Roll, p. 73

Beverages

NUT MILK

1 cup nuts (blanched almonds, cashews, pecans, etc.)
3 cups water

Grind the nuts in a blender or food processor until finely powdered; add the water and blend for 3 minutes. Strain, if desired, and reserve the nut pulp for cereal or baking. Use in place of dairy milk. Serve hot or cold. Makes 1 quart.

Note: when serving nut milk as a beverage or with cereal, etc., add:

Sweetener to taste (barley malt, carob, rice syrup, maple syrup, apple juice concentrate)
1 tsp. vanilla extract

FRESH FRUIT SMOOTHIES

In a blender or food processor, place the suggested fruit combinations (or experiment with your own); add 1 Tbsp. unsweetened protein powder, if desired, and blend until smooth. Add crushed ice or seltzer water, and serve. Each combination makes about 1 cup.

Note: peel overripe bananas before freezing in a plastic bag or freezer container.

1. ½ banana, frozen
   3 strawberries, frozen
   ½ cup apple juice

2. $\frac{1}{2}$ cup skim milk or NUT MILK p. 41
   2 tsp. plain yogurt, optional
   $\frac{1}{2}$ tsp. vanilla extract
   $\frac{1}{2}$ papaya, banana, peach, mango or a similar fleshy
      fruit
   Cinnamon to taste
3. 1 cup unsweetened pineapple juice, chilled
   $\frac{1}{2}$ banana, frozen
4. 1 cup fresh pineapple chunks
   $\frac{1}{2}$ cup strawberries, frozen
5. 1 cup seedless grapes
   $\frac{1}{4}$ cup blueberries
   $\frac{1}{2}$ tsp. vanilla extract
6. $\frac{1}{2}$ cup fresh orange juice
   $\frac{1}{4}$ cup fresh grapefruit juice
   $\frac{1}{2}$ cup fresh pineapple chunks
   A sprinkle of freshly grated coconut
7. 1 cup cherries, pitted
   1 peach, pitted
   1 nectarine, pitted
8. $\frac{1}{2}$ cup apple juice
   2 apricots, pitted
   2 plums, pitted
   $\frac{1}{2}$ cup cherries, pitted
   $\frac{1}{2}$ banana
9. 2 Tbsp. lemon juice
   2 Tbsp. lime juice
   $\frac{1}{4}$ cup tangerine juice
   $\frac{1}{2}$ cup orange juice concentrate
   $\frac{1}{2}$ tsp. vanilla extract
   $\frac{1}{4}$ cup apple juice concentrate, or to taste
10. $\frac{1}{3}$ cup apple juice
    $\frac{1}{3}$ cup apricot nectar
    3 fresh apricots or 6 presoaked, dried apricots
    $\frac{1}{2}$ apple
    $\frac{1}{2}$ tsp. vanilla extract

11. 1 cup coconut milk or NUT MILK p. 41
    $\frac{1}{4}$ cup raspberries
    2 Tbsp. plain yogurt, optional
    $\frac{1}{2}$ tsp. vanilla extract
12. 1 cup fresh orange juice
    1 Tbsp. natural cranberry concentrate
    1 tsp. lemon juice
    Sprinkle of cinnamon
13. $\frac{1}{2}$ ripe banana
    $\frac{1}{2}$ tsp. peanut butter (see NUT BUTTER p. 62)
    1 Tbsp. carob powder
    1 cup low-fat milk or NUT MILK p. 41
14. $\frac{1}{2}$ cup apple juice
    $\frac{1}{2}$ cup unsweetened prune juice
    1 tsp. cashew butter (see NUT BUTTER p. 62)
    1 tsp. plain yogurt, optional
15. 1 cup fresh pineapple chunks
    1 Tbsp. natural, unsweetened black cherry concentrate
    $\frac{1}{4}$ cup fresh orange juice
16. $\frac{1}{2}$ cup apple juice
    $\frac{1}{2}$ cup raspberries
    1 Tbsp. fresh lime juice
17. 1 cup coconut milk
    1 medium peach, pitted
    2 Tbsp. plain yogurt, optional
    $\frac{1}{2}$ tsp. vanilla extract
18. $\frac{1}{4}$ cup chamomile tea (1 tsp. loose chamomile or 1 tea bag steeped in 1 cup boiling water)
    $\frac{1}{2}$ Tbsp. plain yogurt, optional
    2 Tbsp. unsweetened pineapple juice
19. $\frac{1}{4}$ cup peppermint tea (1 tsp. fresh peppermint leaves or 1 tea bag steeped in 1 cup boiling water)
    1 cup apple juice
    1 Tbsp. fresh lemon juice
20. $\frac{1}{4}$ cup fennel tea (1 Tbsp. crushed fennel seeds

steeped in 1 cup boiling water)
$\frac{1}{4}$ cup fresh orange juice
$\frac{1}{2}$ cup raspberries or strawberries
$\frac{1}{4}$ cup sparkling water

FRUIT SODA

1-2 Tbsp. unsweetened frozen or bottled fruit juice
concentrate (apple, apricot, black cherry, cranberry,
grape, orange, pineapple, strawberry, etc., or a combination)
1 cup sparkling water (naturally carbonated)
Crushed ice

Place the concentrate in a tall glass; stir in the sparkling
water. Add the crushed ice and serve with a slice of fresh
fruit. Serves 1.

RAW VEGIE JUICES

For these recipes, a juicer rather than a blender or food
processor makes a great difference in the taste and
texture of the juices. Wash any of the suggested
vegetable combinations (or experiment with your own
combinations) and process in the juicer. Adjust the
seasoning – add sea salt or herb seasoning salt and
freshly ground pepper to taste – and enjoy. Try adding
different kinds of sprouts for variety. Each combination
makes about 1 cup.

1. $\frac{1}{2}$ medium cucumber
   1 organic carrot
   2 stalks celery
   Lemon juice
2. 1 tomato
   1 slice green pepper
   $\frac{1}{2}$ cucumber
   1 stalk celery

    1 green onion
    ½ cup alfalfa sprouts
3. 2 large tomatoes
    3 stalks celery
4. 2 large organic carrots
    2 stalks celery
5. 2 large organic carrots
    ½ cucumber
6. 1 cucumber
    12-15 fresh green beans
    3 radishes
    Lemon juice
7. 1 large tomato
    ½ cup watercress
    Lemon juice
8. 1 large tomato
    2 stalks celery
    ½ large organic carrot
    Small bunch watercress
    1 large sprig parsley
    Squeeze fresh lemon
9. 2 tomatoes
    1 large sprig parsley
    1 green onion
    1 small stalk celery
10. 2 tomatoes
    ½ cup sauerkraut
    1 large sprig parsley

Salads

BLACK-EYED PEA SALAD

½ cup chopped celery
½ cup chopped green pepper
½ cup sliced green onions

1 medium-sized hot pepper, chopped
4 cups cooked black-eyed peas
1 large tomato, coarsely chopped
ITALIAN DRESSING p. 55

In a large bowl, combine all the ingredients and mix well. Chill for at least 1 hour (the longer, the better!). Adjust the seasoning and serve on a bed of lettuce with a garnish of fresh parsley. Serves 6-8.

BLENDED SALAD

1 carrot
1 stalk celery
½ green or red bell pepper
½ cucumber
Small bunch parsley
10 romaine lettuce leaves
1 tomato
Any other favorite vegetables
MISO DRESSING II p. 55

In a food processor, separately prepare the following: grate the carrot; chop the firm vegetables together (celery, peppers, cucumber, parsley); chop the lettuce, a few leaves at a time, then the tomato. Toss all the vegetables together. Add MISO DRESSING II; toss again and top with garbanzo or other beans, nuts, seeds, grated cheese, etc. Serves 4.

CARROT-RAISIN SALAD

4 medium carrots, grated
½ cup raisins
½ cup shredded unsweetened coconut
2 Tbsp. lemon juice
¼ cup TOFU MAYONNAISE p. 56
1 tsp. celery seeds, optional

2 Tbsp. apple juice concentrate, optional

Combine all the ingredients in a large bowl and toss well. Chill and serve on a bed of lettuce leaves. Serves 6-8.

CONFETTI BEAN SALAD

1 cup cooked kidney beans
1 cup cooked garbanzo beans
1 cup cooked green beans, cut in 1-inch pieces
1½ cups cooked corn kernels
½ cup chopped green pepper
½ cup chopped sweet red pepper
½ cup sliced celery
¼ cup sliced green onions
FRENCH LEMON p. 54 or ITALIAN DRESSING p. 55.

Combine all the ingredients in a large bowl and toss gently until well coated with the dressing of choice. Cover and refrigerate several hours or overnight. Serve on a bed of lettuce. Serves 6-8.

COOKED VEGETABLE SALADS

The following salad suggestions make use of chilled pre-cooked vegetables, thus providing a tasty way to use leftovers. Be experimental with the salad greens; try different types of lettuce, spinach, parsley and other fresh herbs, sorrel, Swiss chard, endive, etc. Combine the ingredients for each salad and toss gently with the suggested dressing or one of your favorite dressings. Experiment with your own leftover combinations. Each combination serves 4-6.

1. 2 cups cooked French green beans
   2 cups steamed celery slices
   4 cups chopped salad greens
   FRENCH LEMON DRESSING p. 54 to taste

47

2. 2 cups steamed fresh asparagus
   2 cups chopped watercress
   3 cups chopped romaine lettuce
   MUSTARD DRESSING p. 56 to taste
3. 2 cups steamed celery slices
   ½ lemon, very thinly sliced
   2 cups julienne-cut cooked beets
   3 cups salad greens
   EASY SESAME DRESSING p. 54 to taste
4. 1 cup grated steamed carrots
   1 cup grated steamed beets
   ½ cup chopped cucumber
   ½ cup cooked garbanzo beans
   ½ cup HERB CROUTONS p. 54
   4 cups salad greens
   CUCUMBER DRESSING p. 53 to taste

EASY BEAN SALAD

2 cups fresh green beans, steamed tender-crisp
2 cups kidney beans, cooked
2 cups fresh wax beans, steamed tender-crisp
1 Tbsp. minced fresh parsley or 2 tsp. dried parsley
1 tsp. minced fresh basil or ½ tsp. dried basil
1 tsp. minced fresh oregano or ½ tsp. dried oregano
1 tsp. dried mustard
3 Tbsp. apple juice concentrate
1 Tbsp. rice vinegar
¼ cup lemon juice
⅓ cup cold pressed olive oil
Sea salt and freshly ground pepper to taste

Place all the beans in a large mixing bowl. Combine the remaining ingredients in a screw-top jar and shake well; pour over the beans and toss. Chill well before serving in a bed of lettuce. Serves 4-6.

FRESH FRUIT CUP

2 Tbsp. frozen orange juice concentrate
1 tsp. fresh lemon juice
1 apple, diced
1 orange, peeled and sliced
1 peach, diced
1 banana, sliced
½ cup *each* seedless grapes and blueberries
Any other fruits in season (papaya, mango, grapefruit, etc.), diced or sliced
CURRIED FRUIT DRESSING p. 53, optional
Chopped walnuts or pecans and fresh mint

Combine the juices and prepared fruit in a covered bowl; mix well and chill until ready to serve. Top with the dressing, if desired, and garnish with the walnuts and fresh mint. Serves 6-8.

GARBANZO SALAD

3 cups cooked garbanzo beans (chickpeas)
2 Tbsp. cold pressed olive oil
3 Tbsp. rice vinegar
Pinch of sea salt
6 red radishes
1 small cucumber
2 stalks celery
½ cup watercress
1 Tbsp. fresh parsley, finely chopped
2 tsp. fresh or 1 tsp. dried mint, chopped
1 pint alfalfa sprouts or lettuce leaves
8 black olives
Watercress for garnish

Combine the oil, vinegar and salt; add the chickpeas and marinate overnight. About an hour before serving, slice and dice the vegetables to the size of the garbanzos. Stir

49

into the beans along with the parsley and mint. Place the salad on a bed of sprouts or lettuce and garnish with olives and whole watercress. Serve with pita bread.

JERUSALEM ARTICHOKE SALAD

6 Jerusalem artichokes, grated
2 carrots, grated
3 stalks celery, finely chopped
¼ cup chopped fresh parsley
½ cup TOFU MAYONNAISE p. 56 (more to taste)
Sweetener to taste
Lettuce leaves
¼ cup sliced black olives and a sprig of parsley

Prepare the vegetables and set aside. Combine the parsley, TOFU MAYONNAISE and sweetener; toss with the vegetables. Serve on a bed of lettuce leaves and garnish with black olives and parsley. Serves 6.

STUFFED BEETS

8 fresh medium-sized beets
2 Tbsp. cold pressed oil
2 Tbsp. lemon juice or wine vinegar
1 tsp. Dijon-style mustard
Sea salt and pepper to taste
½ cup sour cream or LOW-FAT 'SOUR CREAM' p. 62
1½ Tbsp. prepared horseradish, drained
½ tsp. Dijon-style mustard

Wash the beets well and cook, unpeeled, in salted, boiling water for 30 minutes. Cool, peel and level off the bottom of the beets so that they will stand up straight. Scoop out the center of each beet, leaving a shell about ¼-inch thick. Save the beet centers and chop finely to use in the stuffing. Mix the oil, lemon, 1 tsp. mustard, salt and pepper together and marinate the beets in this dressing for about 1 hour, turning frequently. Meanwhile, combine the sour cream, horseradish, $\frac{1}{2}$ tsp. mustard and chopped beet centers; season to taste and mix well. Just before serving, drain the beets; fill the centers with the sour cream mixture. Serve 2 stuffed beets on a bed of lettuce for each person. Serves 4.

TOFU EGG(LESS) SALAD I

1 lb. tofu
3 Tbsp. Dijon-style mustard
1-2 tsp. curry powder
1 tsp. dried or 2 tsp. fresh basil
$\frac{1}{3}$ cup TOFU MAYONNAISE p. 56
2-3 green onions, chopped
2-3 stalks celery, chopped
$\frac{1}{4}$ cup chopped fresh parsley
1 tsp. herb seasoning salt or $\frac{1}{2}$ tsp. sea salt
Freshly ground pepper to taste

In a large bowl, crumble the tofu; add the remaining ingredients and mix well. Serve as a tomato stuffing, a dip for crackers or in a pita bread sandwich with lettuce and tomato. Serves 4.

TOFU EGG(LESS) SALAD II

1 lb. tofu
3 Tbsp. Dijon-style mustard
3 Tbsp. diced sweet red pepper
8-10 green olives, chopped
$\frac{1}{3}$ cup TOFU MAYONNAISE p. 56
2 green onions, chopped
2-3 stalks celery, chopped
Herb seasoning salt or sea salt and freshly ground pepper to taste

Crumble the tofu; add the remaining ingredients and

mix well. Serve as a tomato stuffing, a dip for crackers or in pita bread with lettuce and tomato. Serves 4.

TOFU EGG(LESS) SALAD III

1 lb. tofu, crumbled
¼ cup TOFU MAYONNAISE p. 56
1 Tbsp. *each* tamari and Dijon-style mustard
⅛ tsp. *each* ground cumin and tumeric
¼ tsp. paprika
1 green onion, minced
¼ cup *each* chopped celery and green pepper
¼ cup grated carrot

Combine all the ingredients and mix well. Serve as a stuffing for fresh tomatoes or green pepper or top with alfalfa sprouts in a sandwich. Makes about 3 cups.

VEGETABLE ASPIC

2 Tbsp. cold pressed oil
½ cup chopped onion
1 28-oz. can peeled, crushed tomatoes
1 bay leaf
1 clove of garlic, minced or ⅛ tsp. garlic powder
¼ tsp. paprika
½ cup agar-agar flakes
2 Tbsp. tamari
1 Tbsp. cider or rice vinegar
Juice and grated peel from ½ lemon
½ cup diced green pepper
½ cup grated carrot
½ cup chopped celery
½ cup chopped cucumber, radishes, olives or any other
  vegetables
Sea salt and pepper to taste
Small bunch of watercress

In a large skillet, heat the oil and sauté the onions until transparent. Add the tomatoes, bay leaf, garlic and paprika; cook gently for 10 minutes. Add the agar-agar to the tomato mix, and continue to cook for at least 5 more minutes, stirring continuously. Add the tamari, vinegar, lemon peel and juice and chopped vegetables; season to taste. Pour into a large oiled ring mold and cool; chill in the refrigerator for several hours. When ready to serve, turn the aspic out of the mold onto a bed of lettuce, and fill the center with fresh watercress. Serve with TOFU MAYONNAISE p. 56 or MISO DRESSING II p. 55. Serves 6-8.

Salad Dressings, Miscellaneous

CUCUMBER DRESSING

1½ cups chopped cucumber
¾ cup TOFU MAYONNAISE p. 56
2 Tbsp. chopped green onions
1 Tbsp. fresh lemon juice
½ tsp. dill weed
½ tsp. herb seasoning salt or ¼ tsp. sea salt
Vegetable stock to thin

Combine all the ingredients in a blender or food processor and blend until smooth; add the vegetable stock as needed, to thin. Chill for several hours and serve over salad greens. Makes 2 cups.

CURRIED FRUIT DRESSING

1 cup TOFU MAYONNAISE p. 56
⅓ cup apple juice concentrate
⅓ cup mashed peaches, nectarines or plums
½ tsp. curry powder
½ tsp. grated lemon peel

⅛ tsp. sea salt
⅛ tsp. cayenne pepper, optional

Combine all the ingredients in a blender or food processor and blend well. Chill for several hours before serving to blend the flavors. Serve over FRESH FRUIT CUP p. 49 or other fruit salads. Makes 1¾ cups.

EASY SESAME DRESSING

½ cup cold pressed oil
⅓ cup fresh lemon juice (more to taste)
2 tsp. chopped fresh parsley
1 tsp. mixed Italian herbs
1 Tbsp. finely ground toasted sesame seeds
Herb seasoning salt or sea salt to taste

Combine all the ingredients in a screw-top jar with an ice cube; shake well. Remove the ice cube and serve. Makes about ¾ cup.

FRENCH LEMON DRESSING

⅓ cup cold pressed oil
½ cup fresh lemon juice
1 tsp. grated lemon peel
2 Tbsp. cider or rice vinegar
2 tsp. dry mustard
1 Tbsp. apple juice concentrate
1 tsp. miso (soy paste)
¼ tsp. ground white pepper

Combine all the ingredients in a screw-top jar; shake well and chill. Shake again before serving over salad greens. Makes 1 cup.

HERB CROUTONS

Cut whole-grain bread slices into ½-inch cubes. Melt

butter in a skillet and add the bread cubes. Toss the cubes continuously until all sides are browned and crisp; add chopped parsley, garlic powder, Parmesan cheese or any herbs that complement the soup or salad with which they will be served.

ITALIAN DRESSING

$\frac{1}{3}$ cup fresh lemon juice
2 Tbsp. brown rice vinegar
$\frac{1}{4}$ cup cold pressed oil
2 Tbsp. apple juice concentrate
2 Tbsp. water
$\frac{1}{2}$ tsp. mixed Italian herbs
$\frac{1}{8}$ tsp. granulated kelp
$\frac{1}{2}$ tsp. powdered vegetable broth
$\frac{1}{8}$ tsp. onion powder
$\frac{1}{8}$ tsp. garlic powder
Sea salt or herb seasoning salt and pepper to taste

Combine all the ingredients in a screw-top jar; shake well and chill before serving. Use as a salad dressing or marinade for cooked or raw vegetables. Makes about $\frac{3}{4}$ cup.

MISO DRESSING II

$\frac{1}{3}$ cup miso
$\frac{1}{3}$ cup tahini
$\frac{1}{4}$ cup lemon juice
$\frac{3}{4}$-1 cup vegetable stock
1 clove garlic, minced or $\frac{1}{4}$ tsp. garlic powder, optional

Whisk all the ingredients together until smooth and chill well before serving. Makes $1\frac{1}{4}$ cups.

MUSTARD DRESSING

1 cup TOFU MAYONNAISE below or plain yogurt
1½ Tbsp. Dijon-style mustard
1 tsp. prepared horseradish
¼ cup vegetable stock to thin
¼ tsp. herb seasoning salt or ⅛ tsp. sea salt
⅛ tsp. ground white pepper

Whisk all the ingredients together until smooth and chill well before serving. Makes 1¼ cups.

TOFU MAYONNAISE

1 lb. tofu
⅓ cup cold pressed oil
⅓ cup lemon juice
1 Tbsp. brown rice vinegar
½ tsp. onion powder
½ tsp. dry mustard
1 tsp. herb seasoning salt or ½ tsp. sea salt
⅛ tsp. garlic powder or to taste
1 tsp. apple juice concentrate
(Italian herbs to taste for variety)

Blend the tofu in a food processor until smooth; add the oil, lemon juice and seasonings and blend. Add more oil or lemon juice or a little water to adjust the consistency. Makes about 2½ cups.

Sandwich Combinations

These combinations are designed to provide nutritional and protein balance when served on whole-grain bread or toast or tucked into pita bread (a Middle Eastern pocket bread). Many are delicious served cold, while others may be heated to blend the flavors or melt the cheese.

1. Almond butter (see NUT BUTTER p. 62) and apple slices.
2. Cashew butter (see NUT BUTTER p. 62), mixed with raisins, topped with banana slices.
3. CURRIED CASHEW SPREAD p. 59, sliced tomato and onion, topped with alfalfa sprouts.
4. GREAT NORTHERN BEAN SPREAD p. 60, sliced tomato and alfalfa sprouts.
5. HOMMUS p. 61, mixed with chopped fresh spinach, topped with sliced cucumber and red onion.
6. HOMMUS p. 61, sliced avocados and olives, and fresh spinach leaves.
7. HOMMUS p. 61, sliced tomato and cucumber, topped with alfalfa sprouts.
8. LOW-FAT 'CREAM CHEESE' p. 62, apple slices and chopped watercress.
9. LOW-FAT 'CREAM CHEESE' p. 62, mixed with chopped nuts and dried apricots.
10. LOW-FAT 'CREAM CHEESE' p. 62, mixed with chopped green onions, topped with thinly sliced radishes.
11. LOW-FAT 'CREAM CHEESE' p. 62, mixed with chopped olives and walnuts.
12. LOW-FAT 'CREAM CHEESE' p. 62, mixed with chopped pimentos, topped with sliced onion.
13. LOW-FAT 'CREAM CHEESE' p. 62, watercress and sliced tomato.
14. LOW-FAT 'SOUR CREAM' p. 62, mixed with chopped peaches, apples and walnuts.
15. LOW-FAT 'SOUR CREAM' p. 62, mixed with chopped watercress, topped with tomato and cucumber slices.
16. LOW-FAT 'SOUR CREAM' p. 62, mixed with grated, cooked beets and topped with sliced onion and sprouts.
17. LOW-FAT 'SOUR CREAM' p. 62, mixed with sautéed mushrooms, topped with alfalfa sprouts.

18. LOW-FAT 'SOUR CREAM' p. 62, sliced avocado, tomato and onion.
19. Peanut butter (see NUT BUTTER p. 62), mixed with chopped olives and celery, topped with grated carrots and sliced onion.
20. Peanut butter (see NUT BUTTER p. 62), mixed with grated carrots and seedless raisins.
21. Peanut butter (see NUT BUTTER p. 62), topped with grated carrots and sliced bananas.
22. Peanut butter (see NUT BUTTER p. 62), topped with thinly sliced cucumber and tomato.
23. Tahini (sesame butter) and sliced fresh or dried fruit.
24. TOFU MAYONNAISE p. 56 and BLENDED SALAD p. 46, topped with sliced onion.
25. TOFU MAYONNAISE p. 56, mashed avocado, a squeeze of lemon and sliced onion.
26. TOFU MAYONNAISE p. 56, steamed asparagus spears, sliced tomato and alfalfa sprouts.
27. TOFU MAYONNAISE p. 56, mixed with finely chopped onions and celery, topped with alfalfa sprouts.
28. TOFU MAYONNAISE p. 56, mixed with grated carrots, chopped celery and sliced olives.
29. TOFU MAYONNAISE p. 56, mixed with horseradish and mustard, layered with lettuce and slices of onion, cooked beets, cucumber, tomato and green pepper.
30. TOFU MAYONNAISE p. 56, mixed with horseradish layered with sliced avocado and tomatoes, topped with alfalfa sprouts.
31. TOFU MAYONNAISE p. 56, mixed with shredded cabbage and grated carrot, layered with onion and green pepper rings, topped with sliced cheese.
32. TOFU MAYONNAISE p. 56, SCRAMBLED TOFU I or II, p. 63, topped with sliced tomato and onion.
33. TOFU MAYONNAISE p. 56 and thin apple slices, topped

with sliced rennetless Cheddar cheese and toasted.

Savory Snacks

CELERY STUFFING

1 cup LOW-FAT 'CREAM CHEESE' p. 62
½ cup chopped olives
1 Tbsp. minced sweet red pepper
Celery stalks, cut into 3-inch pieces

Mix the cream cheese and chopped olives together well. Stuff generously into the hollow sides of the celery sticks. Makes at least 1 dozen celery pieces.

CURRIED CASHEW SPREAD

2 cups cashew pieces
1-2 Tbsp. curry powder
1½ cups vegetable stock
1 cup cooked brown rice
1 Tbsp. tamari
¼ tsp. onion powder
1 tsp. sea salt
1 Tbsp. lemon juice
¼ tsp. cayenne pepper

In a large skillet or toaster oven, toast the cashews over low heat, until lightly browned; allow to cool. In a food processor, blend the cooled nuts into cashew butter. Add the curry powder, rice and vegetable stock; blend until smooth. Add the remaining ingredients and blend well. Serve as a dip or spread. Makes about 3 cups.

FRESH VEGETABLE PLATTER

Tomato wedges
Sliced cucumbers
Carrot sticks or curls
Celery sticks
Radish flowers
Sliced summer squash
Cauliflower and broccoli flowerettes, lightly steamed
Sliced cooked beets
Whole mushrooms
Red and green pepper rings
Any other favorite vegetables

Arrange the vegetables attractively on a large platter, varying color and shape. Serve with a variety of dips (TOFU-DILL, CURRIED CASHEW, HOMMUS, etc. see pp. 59-65).

GREAT NORTHERN BEAN SPREAD

4 cups cooked Great Northern beans
Vegetable stock, as needed
½ sweet red pepper, chopped
2 green onions, chopped
1 stalk celery, chopped
1-2 Tbsp. cold pressed oil
⅛ tsp. dried or ¼ tsp. minced fresh basil
¼ tsp. dried or ½ tsp. minced fresh parsley
Garlic powder to taste
Onion powder to taste
¼ cup liquid soy protein or 2 Tbsp. tamari
1 cup cooked brown rice

In a food processor or blender, purée half of the beans, adding a little vegetable stock as needed to blend. Meanwhile, in a large skillet, sauté the chopped vegetables in the oil until tender; stir in the herbs and liquid soy protein or tamari. Add the puréed beans, the remaining whole beans and the rice; mix well and simmer until the mixture has thickened into a paste. Chill and serve as a sandwich spread, a dip for crackers or fresh vegetables, or as a stuffing for fresh tomatoes or green peppers. Makes about 4 cups.

HOMMUS

3 cups cooked garbanzo beans (chickpeas)
2 cloves garlic, minced
$\frac{1}{3}$ cup fresh lemon juice
1 tsp. sea salt or to taste
$\frac{1}{2}$ cup tahini (sesame seed paste)
2 Tbsp. cold pressed oil
$\frac{1}{3}$ cup chopped fresh parsley
$\frac{1}{2}$ cup plain yogurt, optional

Blend all the ingredients in a food processor or blender until smooth and creamy. Serve as a spread for crackers, a filling for pita bread or a dip for a FRESH VEGETABLE PLATTER p. 60. Makes 4 cups.

HORSERADISH DIP

1 cup cooked beets, drained
1 tsp. powdered vegetable broth
2 Tbsp. vegetable stock
1 Tbsp. powdered horseradish
1 tsp. cider or rice vinegar
$\frac{1}{4}$ tsp. onion powder
$\frac{1}{4}$ tsp. garlic powder
$\frac{1}{4}$ tsp. dry mustard
Sea salt to taste

Combine all the ingredients in a blender or food processor and blend until smooth. Serve with crackers, chips, or raw vegetables. Makes about $1\frac{1}{4}$ cups.

Phase III: Recipes for Ex-Smokers

LOW-FAT 'CREAM CHEESE'

1½ cups low-fat cottage cheese
¼ cup buttermilk or yogurt
¼ cup skim milk
1 Tbsp. instant non-fat dry milk

In a blender or food processor, combine all the ingredients and blend until very smooth. Cover and refrigerate until thickened into a cream cheese consistency. Makes 2 cups.

LOW-FAT 'SOUR CREAM'

½ cup skim milk
½ cup farmer's, ricotta or low-fat cottage cheese

In a blender or food processor, blend the cheese and milk to the desired consistency. Serve whenever sour cream would be appropriate. Makes 1 cup.

NUT BUTTER

2 cups raw or lightly toasted nuts (cashews, blanched almonds or peanuts)
Sea salt to taste, optional

Chop the nuts in a food processor or grinder and process to the desired consistency. (The longer the processing, the more oil is released.) Add salt if desired, and blend again. Makes about 1½ cups.

SUPER SNACK

¼ cup *each* cashews, almonds and peanuts
¼ cup *each* sesame, sunflower and pumpkin seeds

Combine the nuts and seeds and toast lightly or serve raw. Sprinkle with a little herb seasoning salt, if desired, and keep on hand for a snack. Makes 1½ cups.

62

SCRAMBLED TOFU I

1 Tbsp. cold pressed oil
¼ cup chopped green onions with tops
1 lb. tofu, crumbled
¼ cup cooked carrots, minced
⅛ tsp. garlic powder
½ tsp. dried or Dijon-style mustard
Sea salt and pepper to taste

In a large skillet, sauté the green onions in the oil. Add the remaining ingredients and mix well. Sauté until well heated. Garnish with fresh parsley and serve like scrambled eggs, with whole-grain toast or rice. Serves 2.

SCRAMBLED TOFU II

1 Tbsp. cold pressed oil
¼ cup chopped green onions with tops
¼ cup chopped celery
1 lb. tofu, crumbled
1 tsp. curry powder
½ tsp. tumeric powder
Cayenne pepper to taste
Garlic powder to taste
Sea salt and pepper to taste

In a large skillet, sauté the green onions and celery in the oil. Add the remaining ingredients and mix well. Sauté until well heated. Garnish with fresh parsley and serve like scrambled eggs, with whole-grain toast or rice. Serves 2.

TOFU-DILL DIP

1 lb. tofu
2 Tbsp. lemon juice
2 Tbsp. cold pressed oil

½ tsp. sea salt
½-1 tsp. dill weed or seeds
2 Tbsp. chopped fresh parsley
Pinch of garlic powder

If the tofu is not very fresh, drop it into boiling water for 2-3 minutes; pat dry and blend with the remaining ingredients in a food processor or blender until smooth and creamy. Serve chilled with cut vegetables, chips or crackers. Makes 2 cups.

TOMATO MEXICALI DIP

1 small onion, thinly sliced
4 lb. peeled tomatoes, chopped
1 clove garlic, minced
⅛ tsp. cardamom seeds or powder
½-1 tsp. ground cumin
1 bay leaf
Sea salt and pepper to taste
1 Tbsp. lemon juice or cider or rice vinegar
1 Tbsp. apple juice concentrate
A dash of hot pepper sauce
Chili powder or cayenne pepper to taste
Chopped fresh parsley

In a large skillet, heat a little oil and sauté the onion until tender. Add the tomatoes, garlic, cardamom seeds, cumin, bay leaf, salt and pepper. Simmer, stirring occasionally, for about 30 minutes until the liquid evaporates and the mixture thickens. Strain the purée into a saucepan, to remove the seeds and bay leaf. Add the lemon juice or vinegar, apple juice concentrate, hot sauce and chili powder; bring to a boil, adjust the seasoning to taste and simmer the mixture for a few more minutes. Pour into a serving bowl, sprinkle with chopped parsley and serve hot with crackers or corn chips. Makes about 3 cups.

VEGETABLE GARDEN DIP

1 cup LOW-FAT 'SOUR CREAM' p. 62
¼ cup finely chopped radishes
¼ cup finely chopped green onions
¼ cup finely chopped green pepper
¼ cup finely chopped sweet red pepper
¼ cup finely chopped cucumber
1 clove garlic, minced
½-1 tsp. sea salt
⅛ tsp. ground white pepper
2 tsp. apple juice concentrate, optional

Combine all the ingredients in a small bowl and mix well. Chill and garnish with a sprinkle of paprika or a sprig of fresh parsley. Serve with crackers or a FRESH VEGETABLE PLATTER p. 60. Makes 2 cups.

Sweet Snacks

BAKED APPLES

4 baking apples
2 Tbsp. butter or soy margarine, optional
1 tsp. cinnamon
4 dried figs, chopped
8 dried apricots, chopped
½ cup raisins
¼ cup apple juice concentrate
¼ cup chopped walnuts

Wash and core the apples, leaving ½ inch at the bottom; set aside. Combine the remaining ingredients and mix well. Spoon the stuffing into the cored apples and bake at 350°F. until tender, about 30 minutes. Serves 4.

BANANA-NUT BREAD

4 cups flour (try 2 cups whole wheat, 2 cups unbleached

or 2 cups rice flour, 2 cups unbleached wheat)
1 Tbsp. low-sodium baking powder
1 tsp. baking soda
½-1 tsp. sea salt
1 cup melted butter or soy margarine
½ cup apple juice concentrate
¼ cup maple syrup
2 eggs or equivalent egg replacer
5-6 overripe bananas, mashed
½ cup buttermilk
1 Tbsp. cider or rice vinegar
1 cup chopped walnuts
½ cup raisins or currants

Preheat the oven to 350°F. Sift the dry ingredients together; cut in the butter with a pastry blender. Combine the remaining ingredients; stir into the dry mix. Turn into 2 oiled loaf pans and bake for 45-50 minutes or until a toothpick comes out clean. Cool in the pans for 10 minutes, then turn onto a rack. Makes 2 loaves.

BANANA SHERBET

Peel overripe bananas (allow 1 banana per serving) and freeze overnight in a plastic bag. Chop into ½-inch pieces and blend in a food processor or blender until creamy. Add a little apple juice, if needed, to help blend. Serve in pretty parfait glasses with a strawberry, sprig of mint, slice of orange or nuts as a garnish.

CAROB BROWNIES

⅓ cup maple syrup
2 Tbsp. blackstrap molasses
¼ cup cold pressed oil
2 eggs or equivalent egg replacer

1 tsp. vanilla extract
½ cup *each* rice flour and carob powder
½ cup finely ground sunflower seeds
½ tsp. *each* ginger and cinnamon, optional
½ cup chopped nuts or raisins

Combine the wet ingredients in a large bowl. In another bowl, mix together the dry ingredients; add a little at a time to the wet mixture to make a stiff batter. Stir in the nuts or raisins and turn into an oiled 8-inch pan. Bake at 350°F. for 25 minutes. Cool and cut into squares. Makes 16 brownies.

CAROB CHIP-OATMEAL COOKIES

½ cup butter or soy margarine
¼ cup maple syrup
1 egg or equivalent egg replacer
½ tsp. vanilla extract
1¼ cups flour, sifted (try ¾ cup unbleached wheat, and
    ½ cup brown rice flour)
1 cup oatmeal
¼ tsp. sea salt
2 tsp. low-sodium baking powder
¼ cup carob chips
½ cup raisins
½ cup chopped nuts (pecans or walnuts)

Preheat the oven to 350°F. Melt the butter; add the maple syrup, egg or egg replacer and vanilla and beat until creamy. Sift together the flour, oatmeal, salt and baking powder; stir into the butter mixture. Then add the carob chips, raisins and nuts. Drop the batter by the tablespoonful onto an oiled cookie sheet, about ½-inch apart. Bake for 15 minutes or until golden brown. Makes about 1½ dozen.

CAROB-COATED FRESH FRUIT

Carob coating:
2 Tbsp. butter or soy margarine
¼ cup maple syrup
6 Tbsp. carob powder
¼ cup dairy, soy or NUT MILK p. 41
½ tsp. vanilla extract
A pinch of sea salt

Fruit:
4 ripe bananas, peeled and cut into 1-inch pieces
1 cup finely ground peanuts, optional
or
2 pints fresh strawberries
or
Other fresh fruit of choice

Melt the butter in a small saucepan. Add the maple syrup, carob powder, milk and salt; mix well and simmer for about 5 minutes, stirring continuously. Add the vanilla and stir well; set aside to cool. Dip each piece of fruit into the cooled carob mixture until well coated; roll the bananas in the ground peanuts. Place on wax paper or a buttered platter to set. If the kitchen is too warm for the carob to set properly, place in the refrigerator or freezer until ready to serve as a snack or dessert. Serves 8.

CAROB-PEANUT BUTTER FUDGE BALLS

¼ cup butter or soy margarine
⅓ cup maple syrup
6 Tbsp. carob powder
⅓ cup milk or NUT MILK p. 41 (more if needed)
½-1 cup peanut butter (if unsalted, add ¼ tsp. sea salt)
1 tsp. vanilla extract
2-3 cups oatmeal

In a small saucepan, melt the butter; add the syrup and carob and bring to a boil. Add the milk and simmer for 5 minutes, stirring continuously. Remove from the heat; add the peanut butter and vanilla and mix well. Stir in the oatmeal, 1 cup at a time. Drop by the teaspoonful onto wax paper, cool and serve. Makes 3 dozen balls.

COCONUT MACAROONS

2 Tbsp. maple syrup
¼ cup cashew butter or tahini
Pinch of sea salt
¼ tsp. vanilla extract
2 Tbsp. chopped pecans
1 cup shredded unsweetened coconut
Extra coconut for rolling

Blend the maple syrup, tahini, salt and vanilla together well (add a couple of Tbsp. water if too thick). Stir in the pecans, then the coconut. Form into small balls and roll in the extra coconut until coated. Bake at 350°F. for about 10-15 minutes or until coconut begins to brown. Makes 1½ dozen small balls.

FRUIT-NUT BALLS

½ cup walnuts
½ cup sunflower seeds
1 cup dried currants
½ cup dried figs
½ cup dried dates, pitted
Cinnamon to taste

Combine the walnuts and sunflower seeds in a food processor and chop coarsely. Add the remaining ingredients and chop again; empty into a mixing bowl and mix thoroughly with your hands. Then roll into 1-inch balls and chill until ready to serve. Makes about 2 dozen balls.

GINGER YOGURT

2 cups plain yogurt
1 heaped Tbsp. grated fresh ginger
2 Tbsp. maple syrup
½ tsp. lemon juice, optional
½ tsp. vanilla extract

Combine all the ingredients; mix well, and chill. Serve as a topping for pancakes, waffles, or fresh fruit. Makes about 2 cups.

HOMEMADE APPLESAUCE

6 baking apples
½ cup raisins
½ cup apple juice
1 tsp. cinnamon
1-2 Tbsp. fresh lemon juice

Core and chop the apples; place in large saucepan with the remaining ingredients. Bring to a boil and simmer until well done. Serve with toast, pancakes or waffles or as a main meal side dish. Makes about 3 cups.

MAPLE-CASHEW BUTTER FUDGE

1 cup maple syrup
¾ cup milk or cashew milk (see NUT MILK p. 41)
¼ cup light cream or cashew cream (reduce water – 1:1 nuts to water – in NUT MILK recipe)
2 Tbsp. dry milk powder or finely ground cashews
½ tsp. sea salt
2 Tbsp. soft cashew butter (see NUT BUTTER p. 62)

Combine the syrup, milk, cream and salt in a saucepan and cook briskly for 15 minutes. Remove from the heat, add the cashew butter and beat until smooth and creamy. Pour into a buttered 8-inch pan and cool. Cut into squares. Makes 16 squares.

NUTTY COOKIES

2 cups *each* chopped cashews and pecans
2 cups oatmeal
6 Tbsp. carob powder
1 tsp. baking soda
½ cup butter or soy margarine, melted
1 egg or equivalent egg replacer
1 tsp. vanilla extract
½ cup maple syrup
1 Tbsp. cider or rice vinegar

Combine the dry ingredients in a large mixing bowl. In another bowl, combine the wet ingredients; mix well and stir into the dry mixture. Drop by the teaspoonful onto oiled cookie sheets; bake at 350°F. for 20 minutes. Makes about 3 dozen.

OATMEAL-FRUIT BARS

½ cup butter or soy margarine, melted
¼ cup maple syrup
¼ cup apple juice concentrate
3 eggs or equivalent egg replacer
2 tsp. vanilla extract
2½ cups oatmeal
1 cup flour (unbleached, whole wheat, soy, rice, etc.)
3 tsp. low-sodium baking powder
½ tsp. sea salt
½ cup chopped nuts
½ cup raisins
1 cup combined, chopped dried dates, apricots, and apples

Preheat the oven to 325°F. Combine the wet ingredients

in a small bowl and set aside. In a large mixing bowl, combine the remaining ingredients; add the wet mixture and stir well. Spread in a rectangular baking pan and bake for 30-35 minutes. Cool before cutting into squares. Makes 3 dozen bars.

PEANUT BUTTER COOKIES

¼ cup butter or soy margarine, melted
¼-½ cup maple syrup
1 egg or equivalent egg replacer
1 cup peanut butter
1 tsp. vanilla extract
½ tsp. sea salt (needed only if unsalted peanut butter is used)
½ tsp. baking soda
1 Tbsp. vinegar
2 cups soy flour

Preheat the oven to 375°F. In a large mixing bowl, combine the wet ingredients and beat until smooth. Sift in the dry ingredients and mix well; taste and adjust for desired sweetness. Roll the dough into 1-inch balls and place on an oiled cookie sheet; flatten with a fork and bake for about 15 minutes. Makes about 2 dozen cookies.

RAISIN-SPICE COOKIES

½ cup butter or soy margarine
¼ cup maple syrup
½ tsp. vanilla extract
1 egg or equivalent egg replacer
1¼ cups flour (rice, soy, unbleached, whole wheat)
1 cup oatmeal
¼ tsp. sea salt
½ tsp. low-sodium baking powder
½ tsp. *each* ground cinnamon, ginger, and cardamom
½ cup *each* raisins and chopped nuts (pecans or walnuts)

Melt the butter; add the maple syrup, egg or egg replacer and vanilla and beat until creamy. Sift the flour, salt, baking powder and spices together and stir into the butter mixture. Stir in the raisins and nuts. Preheat oven to 350°F. and set aside for about half an hour. (If the batter is too dry, stir in just a little NUT MILK p. 41.) Then drop by the teaspoonful onto an oiled cookie sheet, about 1 inch apart. Bake for about 15 minutes or until golden brown. Makes about 1½ dozen.

SESAME CANDY

2 Tbsp. sesame oil
1-2 Tbsp. maple syrup
Pinch of sea salt
2 drops vanilla extract
1 cup ground sesame seeds
2 Tbsp. ground almonds

Blend together the oil, syrup, salt and vanilla. Stir in the ground seeds and almonds until thoroughly mixed. Form the mixture into a thin roll and chill. Slice when ready to serve. Makes about 1½ dozen slices.

SESAME HALVAH

1 cup tahini (or sesame butter)
Maple syrup to taste

Stir the tahini until creamy (so the oil is well mixed with the pulp). Add the maple syrup slowly while stirring, until the mixture becomes thick and crumbly and as sweet as desired. Serve on crackers, biscuits, or a sweet bread (challah).

SUNFLOWER SEED ROLL

1 cup ground sunflower seeds
¼ cup chopped nuts

½ cup chopped dried fruit (raisins, dates, apricots, apples, etc.)
1 Tbsp. maple syrup or fruit juice concentrate
⅛ tsp. vanilla extract
Pinch of sea salt
¼ cup nut butter (cashew, almond, tahini, or peanut)

Blend all the ingredients together well. Knead into a ball and form into a roll. Chill and slice when ready to serve. (Or flatten the kneaded ball to ½-inch thickness on a buttered platter; chill and cut into squares.) Makes about 2 dozen pieces.